BANSLED

A Kenyan Adventure

Rawlings Vadanga

In a land far, far away, known as Kenya, found on the African continent, there were three boys who were getting ready to take care of their parents' cattle. The three boys' names were Dishon, Ken and Jerry. Jerry had come to visit his cousin Dishon, at a small village called Bethefage found in Wanondi. Most kids liked to call Dishon 'D.O.' Ken was a friend to both Jerry and D.O. He was also known as the 'big guy.'

On a beautiful Saturday morning, the sun rose up, cutting through the needle leaves of the cypress trees shining on to the green grass, promising a great day.

"Are you ready, boss?" D.O. asked.

"Yes I am!" Jerry responded, "Where are we taking our cattle?"

"Down by the river, to a place called Chifu, boss," D.O. quickly answered.

Jerry had not seen his cousin for almost a year. They were both excited to see each other again. Jerry couldn't wait to take the cattle and find the green pastures. He knew he would have fun.

The three boys led the cattle to the river. It took them about 10 minutes to get there. D.O. told stories of how much had changed since Jerry visited last time. The stories were interesting. The cattle fed on the green grass, drinking water at intervals. The boys rounded up the cattle every time they started to disperse so that the herd could be kept together.

It was almost noon when D.O. suggested moving along the stream. The boys moved the cattle down the stream. When they approached a place called Wamdachi, there was a steep hill with lots of green grass on it. Jerry noticed a trail of exposed ground from the upper side of the hill, all the way down to the small river. At the end of the trail there was a long large fresh banana stalk with three sticks inserted in it.

"What is that?" Jerry asked.

"That is a banana stalk we use to slide down the hill. It's fun. Would you like to try it, boss?"

"Let's do it!"

D.O. explained to everyone how the game worked. Since the banana stalk was heavy, the three boys would have to push it up the hill. The stalk had three sticks inserted in it, which means up to three kids would be able to sit on it, while each of their feet rested on the sticks.

When the stalk was set up on the hill, all the kids would sit on it except for the one who does the pushing. Once the stalk started sliding, the kid pushing it would then jump on to the stalk from the back and slide with the kids. If the stalk slid fast enough it would land in the stream down the hill. If the kids landed in the water, whoever pushed earned one point.

Ken and Jerry sat on the stalk. D.O. pushed, and it started sliding down the hill fast. He jumped on and sat on the moving stalk. The stalk gradually increased its speed as the kids slid down the hill. Sliding down the hill was exciting until it came to a complete stop, almost splashing into the small river.

"That was awesome!" said the big guy.

"Let's do this again," Jerry added, "I really like this game. Since the stalk is from a banana stalk, I would like to name this game Bansled!"

"Just like the sled in the Olympic games?" the big guy asked.

"Yes."

"You are right boss, Bansled sounds good. Let's round up the cattle first, and then slide again."

It was Ken's turn to push the Bansled, while D.O. and Jerry sat on it. Ken pushed the Bansled so hard that he almost fell. He jumped on it. This time it was moving much faster than the first time. The stalk slid so fast that it landed and splashed into the water, with a great sound. The kids laughed and screamed in excitement. All their clothes were wet. They helped each other take the Bansled out of the water and left it on the riverbank. They rested for a few minutes and pushed it up the hill for another round of sliding. It was now Jerry's turn to push it. He did it, however, the stalk moved too fast for him to catch up and jump on.

Ken and D.O. shouted and called for Jerry to run faster, but he could not catch up. The two kids slid downhill on the Bansled while Jerry watched and cheered them.

Next, everyone agreed that the big guy should push it. He pushed the stalk so fast that it landed in the water again. The kids laughed and screamed happily again, cheering at the big splash.

After a few more hours and several slides, all the while keeping an eye on the cattle, it was time to go back home. The big guy won by five points. The kids slowly rounded up the cattle, made sure they drunk enough water and started walking back.

The boys were almost home when a little girl came running happily towards them. The little girl was Jerry's younger sister.

"Hello guys! Why are the backs of your shorts stained?" Vilma
asked.

"We played a game called Bansled," Ken answered.

"Looks like you all had fun, can I come with you next time? Please, Please?"

The boys looked at each other surprisingly while smiling.

"Yes of course!" Jerry answered his younger sister.

They all agreed to take Vilma with them next time.

What is the best adventure you ever had?

_____

_____

_____

_____

_____

_____

_____

_____

_____

If you haven't had one, what is the best adventure you would like to experience?

_____

_____

_____

_____

_____

_____

_____

_____

_____

Color me!
Can you find the map of Kenya below? Color it.

My sincere and special thanks to my son, Leo Vadanga, for inspiring me. I would also like to acknowledge Katharina Janowska, Janine Bitonye, Patricia Gasivwa, Aga Janowska, Peres Vadanga, Reuben Vadanga, Rosemary Vadanga, Kerwin Alliance Asige, Dishon Agade, Britton Bills, Josh Bauman and Martina Mittermüller for their efforts in making the reality of this dream book come true.

9 781736 688113